ENDANGERED!

BEARS

Karen Haywood

 **Marshall Cavendish**
Benchmark
New York

Marshall Cavendish Benchmark
99 White Plains Road
Tarrytown, New York 10591
www.marshallcavendish.us

Editor: Karen Ang
Publisher: Michelle Bisson
Art Director: Anahid Hamparian
Series Designer: Elynn Cohen
Cover Design: Kay Petronio

Library of Congress Cataloging-in-Publication Data

Haywood, Karen Diane.
Bears / by Karen Haywood.
p. cm. — (Endangered!)
Includes bibliographical references and index.
Summary: "Describes the characteristics, behavior, and plight of
endangered bears species, and what people can do to help"—Provided by publisher.
ISBN 978-0-7614-2987-6
1. Bears—Juvenile literature. I. Title.
QL737.C27H42 2008
599.78—dc22
2008011454

Front cover: A giant panda
Title page: A moon bear
Back cover: A grizzly bear (top); A sun bear (bottom)

Photo research by Pamela Mitsakos
Front cover: Gerry Ellis/Minden Pictures
The photographs in this book are used by permission and through the courtesy of: *Alamy:* Terry Whitaker, 1; Arco Images, 6;
Petra Wegner, 9; blickwinkel, 15; Danita Delimont, 21; Juniors Bildarchiv, 25, 38; Photo Network, 26; Steven J. Kazlowski, 28; Nigel
Hicks, 32. *Minden Pictures:* Peter Oxford, 4; E.A. Kuttapan, 19; Michio Hoshino, 34; Konrade Wothe, 40. *Shutterstock:*
Rick Parsons, back cover (top); Alistair Michael Thomas, back cover (bottom); Vova Pomortzeff, 10; oksanaperkins, 22; Mike
Flippo, 43. *Photo Researchers, Inc.:* Terry Whitaker, 13; Andy Rouse, 14; Adam Jones, 16. *AP Images:* Ann Batdorf/Associated
Press, 43; Ken Bohn/Associated Press, 45.

Printed in China
1 2 3 4 5 6

Contents

Introduction

Bears have lived on most of the planet for millions of years. It is possible that early humans observed the behavior of the ancient cave bear. From this animal, the humans learned which plants they could eat and which ones were poisonous.

Bears also play a part in the mythology and religion of different cultures around the world. A well-known constellation, or

collection of stars, is called Ursa Major or "The Great Bear." Ancient Greeks connected this constellation with gods and other beings. Today, most people know Ursa Major as the Big Dipper. American Indians believe that the bear is an important symbol of power. Bear

A scientist puts a special radio collar on an Andean bear cub. The collar will help scientists learn more about these endangered bears and how people can protect bear populations.

designs can be found on their pottery, totem poles, canoes, and blankets.

Long ago, there were many kinds of bears. Over the years, some died out for natural reasons. But there were other **species** of bears to take their place. Now, however, many types of bears are in danger of vanishing from our planet forever. Experts believe that human interference—in the form of over-hunting or **habitat** destruction—is the main reason.

For example, two types of bears are now **extinct** because of humans. The Atlas bear was hunted for sport and the last one is believed to have disappeared from Africa in the 1870s. Now there are no more native bears on that continent. Similarly, all of the Mexican grizzlies are gone. They were poisoned, shot, and trapped to extinction.

Today, several bear species are endangered, or may become extinct. Habitat destruction, over-hunting, and other human interference are the main reasons for this. However, many **conservation** efforts are being made to help the endangered bears. These include creating wildlife **sanctuaries** and passing laws that prevent hunting endangered species. Most importantly, people are trying to learn more about the bears and what else can be done to protect them.

1

Spectacled Bears

This bear is the only bear that is native to South America. Also called the Andean bear, it often lives in regions around the Andes Mountains. The spectacled bear is the last remaining relative of ancient short-faced bears. Now extinct, the short-faced bears once roamed the land that included North, Central, and South America about two million to ten thousand years ago.

This 5-foot-long (1.5-meter-long), 140-pound to 340-pound (63.5-kilogram to 154.2-kilogram) bear gets its name from the rings of pale-colored fur around its eyes. These markings make the spectacled bear look like it is wearing spectacles, or eyeglasses.

Venezuela
Colombia
Equator 0°
Ecuador
ANDES
SOUTH AMERICA
Peru
MTS.
Bolivia

habitat of
spectacled bears

While it can live in the desert, tropical grasslands, and coastal areas, the spectacled bear likes to make its home in cloud forests. These are forests so high up in the mountains that they are actually in the clouds.

Cloud forests provide the fruits and tropical flowers that are the spectacled bear's favorite foods. The bears will also eat berries, grasses, orchid bulbs, cactus flowers, insects, and small animals, such as mice, rabbits, and birds. Because food is plentiful throughout the year, spectacled bears have no need to **hibernate** in the winter like many other bears.

IN DANGER

There are only about 2,000 to 2,400 spectacled bears remaining in the wild today. The bears are losing their habitat because the forests are being destroyed for logging, cattle ranches, and roads. Even though it is illegal to hunt the bears, the law is very difficult to enforce. As a result, these bears are still killed for their body parts, fur, and meat. The spectacled bear's gallbladder—an organ near its stomach—is used in ancient Andean medicine as a cure for blindness and other eye illnesses.

If the spectacled bear is to survive, laws against hunting must be enforced. New national parks and sanctuaries need to be created for these bears.

The spectacled bear spends more time in trees than other bears. It can build a platform out of leaves and branches high in the trees where it sleeps or rests. A spectacled bear may also sleep in an oval-shaped bed that the bear digs into the ground near the base of a cliff.

2

Sun Bears

The sun bear makes its home in the Asian lowland tropical rainforests of Thailand, Myanmar, Malaysia, Sumatra, Laos, Cambodia, Vietnam, and Borneo. These forests are very warm and very rainy.

The bear's name comes from the golden markings on its chest, which many people think looks like the rising or setting sun. The rest of the bear's coat is black or dark brown and its hair is very short and sleek.

Males weigh 60 pounds to 145 pounds (27.2 kg to 65.7 kg) and can grow up to 5 feet (1.5 m) long. Females can

Common nicknames for the sun bear include Malay bear, dog bear, and honey bear.

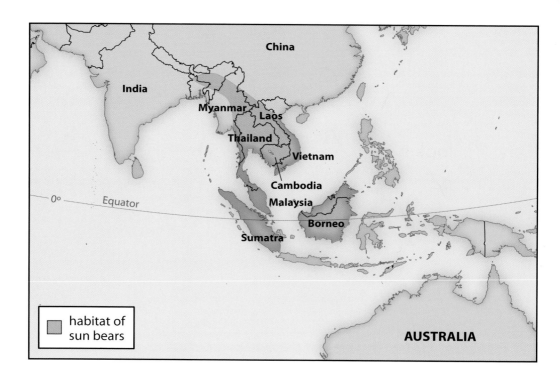

weigh nearly 110 pounds (49.8 kg). It is the smallest of all the bears, but the sun bear may be the most **aggressive,** and may attack more easily. They have strong paws with long, curved claws. Their claws and the bare soles of their paws help make them excellent tree climbers.

Sun bears are best known for their love of honey. They will also eat fruits, berries, insects, termites, birds, eggs, and small animals. As wild food sources become harder to find, sun bears that live near humans show up near communities or on people's property. These bears are hungry and look for food in garbage cans or food storage areas. Sun bears have also been known to eat farmers' crops or feast on the young livestock on ranches. When they are looking for food, the sun bears often damage coconut palm, banana, and cocoa plantations in the region. As a result, many are shot or trapped by angry farmers who are protecting their crops.

One of the ways a bear finds food is by using its nose. A bear's sense of smell is so strong that it can recognize a scent—like the scent of a human—more than fourteen hours after the person walked along a hiking trail.

In different parts of Asia, many sun bears are captured from the wild and kept in small dirty cages in amusement parks.

IN TROUBLE

The sun bear is one of the most endangered bears. Hunters kill sun bears for their gallbladders, which are used in Asian medicine. Sometimes sun bear cubs are captured and sold as pets. Unfortunately, when these cubs become adults they are sold for meat or medicine. Most of the sun bear's rainforest habitat has been destroyed by logging and farming. In addition to destroying the forest and bear trails, logging roads provide easy access for people who enter the forest to hunt the bears.

War and other military actions in many parts of Southeast Asia have affected the lives of sun bears.

When people's homes and lands are destroyed during wars, the surrounding wilderness—and the animals living in it—are also hurt. Parts of the sun bear's natural habitat have also been taken away to make space for military camps. Some experts also say that increased warfare in those regions has allowed more people to own guns that are used to hunt the bears.

It is important for scientists to learn more about these small but interesting bears, and to protect their habitat. It may be possible to reconnect some of the habitat that remains. Some of these efforts are currently under way in places like Vietnam. If the wild sun bears cannot be protected, then the few remaining sun bears may spend the rest of their lives in zoos.

This sun bear family lives in a nature preserve where they are protected from hunters.

3

Sloth Bears

The sloth bear, which is closely related to the sun bear, can live in either a dry forest, a wet rainforest, or in different grasslands, where large rocks, shrubs, and trees provide shelter. The bears are found in parts of Asia, including India, Sri Lanka, and Nepal. Some have been seen in Bhutan and Bangladesh. The wild population of the sloth bear ranges between 10,000 and 25,000 and is quickly declining.

Though sloth bears can weigh nearly 300 pounds (136 kg), they can move very quickly. Some can even run faster than humans!

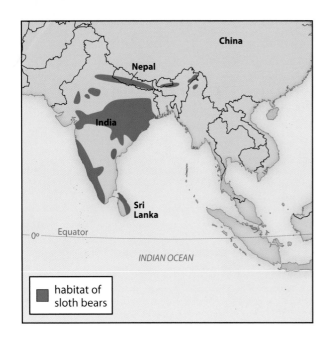

This bear is mostly black and dark brown with long, shaggy hair. There is a white or yellowish patch of fur on its chest in the shape of a U or Y. Its long muzzle has very short, pale hair.

Sloth bears have very large feet and long claws. Adult males grow to be 5 feet to 6 feet (1.5 m to 1.8 m) long, and weigh 175 pounds to 310 pounds (79.3 kg to 140.6 kg). Females are the same length and weigh 120 pounds to 210 pounds (54.4 kg to 95.2 kg).

SLOTH BEAR BEHAVIOR

The sloth bear got its name from explorers who saw them hanging upside down from branches. The explorers thought that bears were like sloths, a type of animal that hangs upside down from trees. Though they can climb trees to find food and shelter, most sloth bears rest in dens or caves. However, unlike many other bears, sloth bears do not need to hibernate in the winter. This is because the weather is usually warm throughout the year, making food easier to find.

Sloth bears eat ants, eggs, flowers, grass, honey, and fruits such as mangoes and figs. Termites are the sloth bear's favorite food, and the bear is an excellent termite hunter. It finds the insects by using its very good sense of smell. Once it locates the insects, the sloth bear rips open the termite nest with its sharp claws. The bear then uses

The mother sloth bear is the only kind of bear that carries her cubs on her back. This may be one reason why the sloth bear's fur is longer and thicker on its back and shoulders.

its long tongue to reach in and grab the termites. A sloth bear can even close its nostrils—the openings on its nose—to keep the termites out!

IN DANGER

Sloth bear populations are declining in the wild, and are threatened with extinction. Humans are the main danger for sloth bears. In many parts of the world, rainforests and other forests in Asia are cut down to make room for human civilization. The trees are also used for wood products. Large termite mounds—which the bears need for food—are also destroyed as humans settle in nearby areas. As a result, the sloth bears have little food and fewer places to live. They sometimes end up too close to human communities, where they destroy crops and property.

Humans have a long history of capturing sloth bears and using them for entertainment. Many of these bears have been caught and forced to perform in circuses or other traveling shows. In 1998, India's government banned the use of sloth bears as dancing bears. Unfortunately, there

The Sloth Bear Welfare and Conservation Project's goal is to end the use of dancing bears in India.

are still thousands of bears being kept for this purpose. There are, however, many organizations that want to help these bears.

There are also programs that are trying to help the sloth bear populations through research and education. Protected land has also been set aside for sloth bears to live freely. Some sloth bears are protected in Nepal's Royal Chitwan National Park and in the Jessore Sloth Bear Sanctuary in India. However, experts agree that in order to survive in the wild, sloth bears will need more safe places to live.

4

Brown Bears

The brown bear has the widest range—or lives in more places on Earth—than any other bear. Within its range, the brown bear can live in many different types of habitats. These include the cold plains, in the **tundra**, the forests, and in some mountain areas. Russia has the largest brown bear population in the world—about 125,000 animals. However, in Europe and Asia these bears are generally found in very small numbers.

In western North America, where the brown bear is usually called a grizzly bear, the population is smaller than 75,000. That is less than 2 percent of what the

Some North American brown bears live near salmon rivers. The bears catch the slippery fish with their powerful paws or in their strong jaws.

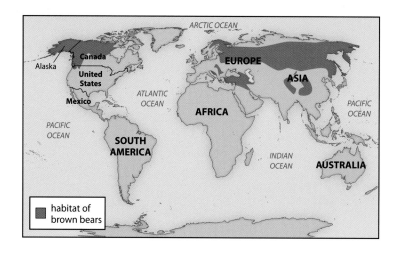

habitat of
brown bears

grizzly population was when European settlers first arrived in North America more than three hundred years ago. Most grizzlies now live in western Canada, Alaska, and in a few of the other western United States.

BROWN BEAR FACTS

A brown bear is very sturdily built. It has a large head with small ears, and long, curved claws. Although its fur is usually brown, it may be almost white, blond, or even black. One way to identify a brown bear is by the hump on its back between its shoulders. This hump is made up of a lot of strong muscles. These muscles give the brown bear its excellent digging skills and powerful striking force in its front paws.

Depending upon the type of brown bear and where it is found, a grown male can weigh anywhere from 300 pounds to 900 pounds (136 kg to 408.2 kg). A female usually weighs between 200 pounds and 455 pounds (90.7 kg to 206.3 kg). Brown bears can be as long—or tall if they are standing up—as 9 feet (2.7 m). An exception is the Kodiak bear. This brown bear is found in Alaska and can grow to

The brown bear's large body can make it look like a slow-moving animal. But these bears can run very fast—between 30 and 35 miles per hour (48.2 and 56.3 kilometers per hour)!

10 feet (3 m) long and weigh more than 1,000 pounds (45.3 kg)! Usually, the heaviest North American brown bears live on the coasts of Alaska and British Columbia in Canada where they can catch and eat salmon, which is a very healthy and fattening meal.

Brown bears are omnivores, which means they eat plant material and meat. Brown bears are also scavengers, which means they eat the bodies of dead animals they find. Scavenging is an important way to find food

Cubs stay with their mother for about three to five years, learning to hunt and behave like adult bears. This is part of the reason why many bear populations are decreasing. Female bears cannot quickly produce enough cubs to replace bears that die or are killed.

in the spring before many plants have begun to grow. Unfortunately, bears also like to hunt for food in garbage dumps and places where food is stored, which makes them more likely to come into contact with humans.

IN DANGER

Over the years, people have killed large numbers of brown bears for food and clothing, for sport, and out of fear. For example, the California grizzly disappeared from the state of California when the last one was shot in 1922. Brown bear habitats are being destroyed to make space for farms, housing developments, and roads. Forests are also cut down to make products such as building materials and paper. As their habitats are taken away, brown bears are more likely to come into contact with people. This can lead to more brown bear deaths.

Today there are many brown bears in parts of Alaska, Canada, and Russia. But in other places their numbers are very small. The grizzly is currently considered a threatened species by the U.S. Fish and Wildlife Service. This means that it is likely to become endangered in the near future throughout all or most of its range.

How can this be prevented? By protecting brown bears from people. For example, there are bear sanctuaries, where the bears can freely roam. One of these is the McNeil River State Game Sanctuary in Alaska. Hunting is usually not allowed in these places and the bears can live in peace.

5

Black Bears

THE AMERICAN BLACK BEAR

The American black bear lives only in North America. American black bears live in forests as far south as Florida and Mexico, and as far north as forests in Alaska and Canada.

While the American black bear usually has a black coat and a brown muzzle, or snout, the fur may be honey-colored, chocolate-brown, cinnamon-brown, pale blue, or even white! The white ones are called Kermode bears and

Fully grown, wild male black bears usually weigh between 125 pounds and 500 pounds (56.6 kg and 226.7 kg). Females are smaller, weighing 90 pounds to 300 pounds (40.8 kg to 136 kg).

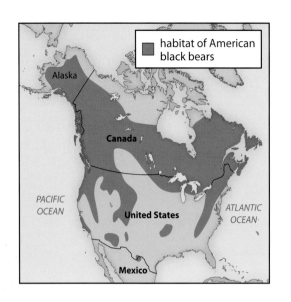

habitat of American black bears

Alaska

Canada

PACIFIC
OCEAN

United States

ATLANTIC
OCEAN

Mexico

live in British Columbia in western Canada. The blue bear is the silvery blue-black glacier bear found in southeastern Alaska and western Canada.

A black bear's claws are short and curved to help it climb quickly. Black bears can climb trees to escape from an enemy, but more often they climb to find food, such as acorns, nuts, berries, fruits, and insects. They may even find some honey in a beehive up in the trees. On the ground, black bears will eat grasses and roots. If none of their favorite food is available, some black bears will eat meat, especially beavers and small rodents. The black bears that live near salmon rivers in Alaska and Canada feast on fish.

Decreasing Numbers

Unfortunately, in some areas American black bears have died out completely. In these regions, their natural forest habitats were destroyed to build roads, to clear land for farms and homes, or to use the trees for wood products. Today there are no black bears left in the Midwest and in many parts of the eastern United States.

The black bear populations in the southeastern United States have been observed since the late 1960s by organizations like the Southern Appalachian Bear Study Group. To protect the black bears, several black bear sanctuaries were created in the 1970s. These were scattered throughout the national forests in North Carolina, Tennessee, and in the Great Smoky Mountains National Park. As a result, population estimates for the black bears in that part of the country remain steady at 2,000 to 2,500 bears.

A STATE MAMMAL

One endangered American black bear is also an official state symbol. In 1992, Louisianans chose the Louisiana black bear as the state mammal. These bears can grow to weigh about 400 pounds (181.4 kg), and once lived in many of Louisiana's forests.

However, by 1992, the bears' population dropped so low that they are now considered endangered. Today Louisianans work hard to protect their state mammal since there are only about four hundred left in the wild.

Asiatic black bears are very bipedal, which means that sometimes they will walk on their two back feet. These bears have been known to walk upright for almost half of a mile, which is quite a long way for a bear!

THE ASIATIC BLACK BEAR

The Asiatic black bear lives in hilly and mountainous regions from the Middle East to Southeast Asia, and eastern Russia, North and South Korea, and Japan. Asiatic black bears generally live in mountain forests. When the weather gets colder, these bears tend to move to the warmer lowlands.

The bear may be black or dark brown with a pale-colored muzzle. The fur around the shoulders and throat of an Asiatic black bear is long and shaggy. The bear has a crescent-shaped white mark on its chest, which gives the bear its other name—the moon bear.

Adult Asiatic black bears can be 4 feet to 6 feet (1.2 m to 1.8 m) in length. Grown males can weigh up to 440 pounds (199.5 kg), while females may

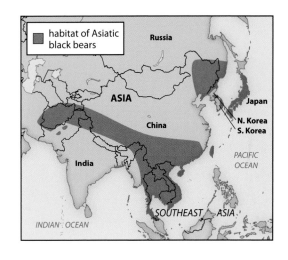

grow to be 275 pounds (124.7 kg). The bear prefers grasses, fruits, berries, seeds, and honey. Sometimes a small part of its diet is made up of meat, mostly in the form of insects. Asiatic black bears are very good tree climbers and can climb high to reach fruits and nuts.

At Risk

Asiatic black bears are often caught and killed to be used for traditional medicine or for special foods, such as bear-paw soup. Because the bears can walk on their hind legs for long periods of time, it is common for cubs to be taken from the wild and sold to a circus or some other traveling show.

Like other bears, the Asiatic black bears are also facing habitat loss. They are being crowded out as humans move into the bears' home ranges. The Asiatic black bear will survive only if laws are passed to protect them in their natural habitat.

Polar Bears

The polar bear's habitat is the Arctic, which includes the land and floating frozen ice masses surrounding the North Pole. The climate in these areas is very cold, but the polar bear is well-adapted to living in such conditions. The bear has a heavy coat of fur. Polar bear fur looks white, but each strand is actually translucent. This means that it is almost clear in color and allows light to pass through it. Sunlight goes through the polar bear fur and onto the skin below, which is black. The dark color allows the skin to absorb light and heat, keeping the polar bear

When hunting for seals, polar bears wait next to breaks in the ice where the seals come up for air. When a seal swims up to breathe, the polar bear quickly uses its huge paws to catch it.

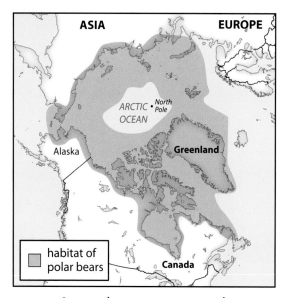

ASIA

EUROPE

ARCTIC
OCEAN
North
Pole

Alaska

Greenland

habitat of
polar bears

Canada

warm in freezing temperatures. The polar bear also has a thick layer of fat beneath the skin, which helps to protect it from the bitter cold.

The polar bear is the largest land carnivore alive today. Standing up straight, a polar bear may be more than 10 feet (3 m) tall. Adult male polar bears usually weigh 880 pounds to 1,500 pounds (399.1 kg to 680.3 kg). Most females usually weigh between 440 pounds and 660 pounds (199.5 kg to 299.3 kg).

Polar bears mainly eat meat, such as seals, fish, young walruses, caribou, small beached whales, and seabirds. During the summer when some plants are available, these bears will eat grasses, berries, kelp, and seaweed.

POLAR BEARS AND PEOPLE

Polar bears have been hunted for hundreds of years by the Native people of the far north—the Inuit of Canada,

Alaska, and Greenland. They called the bear *Nanuk* and believed that it was wise and powerful. The bears' skins were used for clothing and blankets. The bear meat was tasty food for the people and their dogs. Hunting bear was a way of life for these Native peoples, and at first they only killed what they needed to survive.

In the 1700s, however, hunters in the north—some Native and some from other places—realized that selling and trading polar bear skin could be very profitable. For hundreds of years, so many bears were killed that it was feared the bear would become extinct. To help preserve polar bear populations, Russia made polar bear hunting illegal in 1956. In 1973, the polar bear nations—Canada, Denmark, Norway, the United States, and the former Soviet Union (which includes Russia)—signed the Agreement on the Conservation of Polar Bears. This agreement meant that all of those countries had to limit hunting, protect the bear's environment, and do research to learn more about polar bears.

Recently, the United States and Russia signed an additional Agreement on the Conservation and

Conservation efforts have led to tougher laws that protect female polar bears and their young cubs.

Management of the Alaska-Chukotka Polar Bear Population. This improves upon the 1973 agreement by limiting the number of polar bears that are caught each year. The agreement also prevents the hunting of females with cubs, or hunting cubs that are younger than one year old. This treaty was signed in October 2000, but it still has not been ratified, or approved, by the U.S. Senate.

Habitat Destruction

Unfortunately, hunting is not the only threat to polar bear survival. The arctic climate is getting warmer, and the sea ice melts earlier and freezes later. The polar bears need the hardened ice to hunt seals and other food. With less ice, they have less time to hunt for food. When the arctic waters take longer to freeze, female polar bears—who usually give birth in the winter—cannot eat as much as they need to provide for their cubs. Some scientists fear that as more ice melts, the bears will be forced to swim longer distances in search of hardened ice. Polar bears have drowned this way.

Another problem the polar bears face is pollution. Toxic, or poisonous, chemicals have traveled north through wind and ocean currents. These chemicals were used in factories, farms, and other industries. This chemical pollution makes the bears sick and also kills the fish, seals, and other animals that the bears need for food. Pollution in the form of garbage and other waste also hurts arctic animals. Stronger laws and better waste-disposal practices can help to preserve polar bear populations.

Parts of Canada's Hudson Bay are popular places for polar bears to hunt seals on the sea ice. However, the sea ice there now breaks up three weeks earlier than when it did thirty years ago. The polar bear population in the bay has declined, from 1,200 in 1985 to fewer than 950 in 2004. At the current rate, experts predict that polar bears may be extinct in southern Hudson Bay by the year 2050.

7

Giant Pandas

These large bears used to roam through the forests of southern China, Vietnam, and Myanmar. However, nearly half of the natural habitat of these Asian bears disappeared between 1974 and 1988. Today, wild pandas live only in six tiny regions in the southwestern part of China.

PANDA LIVES

Giant pandas live in bamboo forests high up in the mountains where they feed on bamboo plants. In fact,

Male giant pandas grow up to 6 feet (1.8 m) long and weigh 190 pounds to 275 pounds (86.1 kg to 124.7 kg) in the wild. Females are slightly shorter and weigh about 155 pounds to 220 pounds (70.3 kg to 99.7 kg).

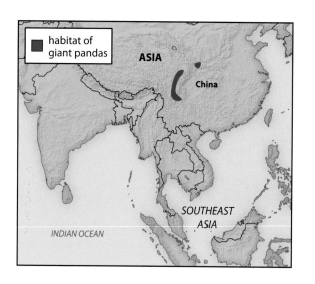

habitat of giant pandas

ASIA

China

SOUTHEAST ASIA

INDIAN OCEAN

99 percent of the panda's diet is bamboo. They may also eat a few other plants and a very small amount of eggs and fish. An adult giant panda eats 36 pounds (16.3 kg) of leaves and stems each day. This means the bear spends most of its day eating.

The giant panda is easy to recognize. It is a sturdy-looking black-and-white bear with small patches of black fur around the eyes. Compared to other bears, a panda's head is large in relation to the rest of its body. The panda's fur is coarse, or rough, and slightly oily. The oil keeps water from reaching the bear's skin, which helps it stay warm in the chilly mountains.

In the wild, pandas usually live by themselves and not in a group or pack like some other mammals. Most wild pandas have a main "home" area that they stay in. This area is about 1 to 2 square miles (2.5 to 5.1 square km) and is marked by each panda's own special scent. Males

Unlike other bears, a panda's front paws have six digits, or fingers. One of these fingers is a wrist bone that acts like a thumb. It helps the animal grasp and control the bamboo branches as it eats.

and females find each other to have babies, but the female panda raises the cub on her own.

A SYMBOL OF ENDANGERMENT

Giant pandas are extremely endangered. Research has shown that there are as few as 3,000 pandas living

Many of the pandas found in zoos in the United States and other countries are actually "borrowed" from Chinese panda breeding programs. To teach more people about the problems these pandas face, the bears are sent to other countries where people can enjoy watching and learning about them. In exchange, these countries send money back to China to be used to preserve and protect more of the wild panda population.

Tai Shan was born in 2005 at the National Zoo in Washington, D.C. His name means "peaceful mountain."

in the wild today. As the human population grows and people continue to cut down the bamboo forests to build houses and farms, the bears' habitats and sources of food are disappearing. Many of the giant pandas that remain in the mountains live in special, protected areas created by the Chinese government.

China is also home to panda breeding and research centers. These centers are dedicated to protecting giant pandas and working to increase panda populations. Scientists and workers at these centers help raise these pandas from birth until young adulthood. During that time, they make sure the pandas

This three-week-old panda weighs only one pound! When baby pandas are born in zoos or breeding centers, they are given special care to make sure they stay healthy.

have enough to eat and a safe place to grow and learn survival skills.

Because of its level of endangerment, the panda has become a symbol for all endangered animals around the world.

If humans do not do more to protect endangered animals, the giant pandas—and other endangered bear species—could disappear forever.

GLOSSARY

aggressive—Being more likely to attack.

bipedal—The ability to walk on two feet.

conservation—The act of preserving or protecting something.

extinct—No longer existing.

habitat—The place where a plant or animal lives or grows.

hibernate—To rest and be inactive for a long period of time. Animals often hibernate during cold months when food is hard to find.

sanctuary—A place that provides shelter or protection.

species—A specific type of animal.

tundra—A treeless plain—usually found in cold regions—that is mostly made up of mosses, lichens, herbs, and very small shrubs.

FIND OUT MORE

Books

Hirschi, Ron. *Lions, Tiger and Bears: Why Are Big Predators So Rare?* Honesdale, PA: Boyds Mills Press, 2007.

Kalman, Bobbie and Kylie Burns. *Endangered Bears*. New York: Crabtree Publishing Co., 2007.

Rosing, Norbert and Elizabeth Carney. *Face to Face with Polar Bears.* Washington, D.C.: National Geographic, 2007.

Thomas, Keltie. *Bear Rescue: Changing the Future for Endangered Wildlife.* Buffalo, NY: Firefly Books, 2006.

Web Sites

American Zoo and Aquarium Association's Bear Den
http://www.BearDen.org

Defenders of Wildlife – Kids' Planet
http://www.kidsplanet.org

Giant Pandas at the National Zoo
http://nationalzoo.si.edu/Animals/GiantPandas/default.cfm

U.S. Fish & Wildlife Service Kids' Corner
http://www.fws.gov/endangered/kids

Organizations

National Wildlife Federation
11100 Wildlife Center Drive
Reston, VA 20190
1-800-822-9919
http://www.nwf.org

World Wildlife Fund
1250 Twenty-Fourth Street, N.W.
P.O. Box 97180
Washington, DC 20090-7180
1-800-960-0993
http://www.worldwildlife.org

INDEX

Pages numbers in **boldface** are illustrations.

ABOUT THE AUTHOR

Karen Haywood has edited and written many books for young readers. She lives in North Carolina where she watches the squirrels steal fruit from the apple trees in her backyard as she writes. Inspired by the first Earth Day in 1970, she has been a strong advocate for the environment and animal rights for many years.